What Floats Your Boat?
The Key to a Fulfilling and Sucessful Life

By E. Lawrence Brock, J.D., Timothy S. Taylor, &
Dawn Brock

Copyright © 2025 by E. Lawrence Brock & Timothy S. Taylor

All rights reserved.

No portion of this book may be reproduced in any form without written permission from the publisher or author, except as permitted by U.S. copyright law.

What Floats Your Boat

This book is dedicated to

Our wives, Joyce and Christine, who have traveled this journey with us. They were always there to help bail out water when needed, trim the sails at the right time, chart a steady course, and enhance all the good times.

The next generations. We hope they find what floats their boat faster than we did.

And

You because no matter where you are or what stage of life you're in, it is always helpful to seek self-improvement.

What Floats Your Boat

Table of Contents

Part 1

Chapter 1 7

Chapter 2 11

Part 2

Chapter 3 17

Chapter 4 19

Chapter 5 26

Chapter 6 37

Chapter 7 44

Part 3

Chapter 8 48

Chapter 9 55

Chapter 10 64

Part 4

Chapter 11 72

Chapter 12 76

Apendix A 90

Apendix B 92

Works Cited 98

About the Authors 99

Part 1

Introduction

Chapter 1

Welcome Aboard

If you're reading this, most likely it is for one of two reasons: One, you saw the boat on the cover and thought, "I love boats! I'm going to buy this book solely on the cover and do no further research," in which case you are bound to be disappointed. We know little about boats except that they should float, and if they don't, then something is wrong. Or two, you're trying to make a change in your life, and you thought this book could help.

If you're in that second group, welcome, we're glad you're here. If you're in that first group, you are also welcome. We hope this helps you, even if it's not what you were looking for. This book will take you through exercises to help you optimize your life and find a way to live a successful and fulfilling life. We acknowledge that the definition of successful and fulfilling can be different for each person, especially when it pertains to one's life. Some people think being successful is making money. Others see it as being generally happy with their day-to-day lives. And still, others might have a completely different definition that we haven't thought about.

Well, good news: our method can help you find success

in whatever way you define it. However, we'd be lying if we didn't say that our main definition of success is being generally happy in your day-to-day life. And we technically can't guarantee you all the money you wish. But in our experience, following this method and in life, if you find happiness in your day-to-day, you often end up being able to make enough money to provide for your needs and most of your wants.

Our goal with this book is to help you. We want you to enjoy your life and feel fulfilled. Which is great, but why should you care if we want that? Who are we? Well, together, we're an attorney, a real estate agent, and a writer. We're ages 75, 59, and 33. And we all have had struggles that we wished we had had this method to help us through. So let us tell you a bit about us.

First, Larry Brock. Larry is an attorney who has been working in the legal system for most of his life. He began working as a photographer for a local paper and, as such, followed many attorneys and legal professionals around to get the perfect shot. He attended, failed out of, reattended, and graduated from law school and passed both the California and Utah State bar exams. Larry has worked in nearly every facet of the law and definitely got trapped in the I'll take whatever case I can because I need the money mindset. Luckily, he was able to escape that mindset and find his passion in helping people. For years, he helped them deal with the legal system after a loved one died. Now, he wants to help people avoid the trap he fell into and find their passion before they get as old as he is.

Tim hasn't always been a real estate agent. For many years,

he worked in the audio/visual world. Unfortunately, that world came crashing down when he was asked to leave his position and denied work at other places due to a noncompete clause he was forced to sign. And as much as we'd like to give all the gory details of that story, we can't. There are still people out there who might wish to do him harm if we say much more. But to say it upended his life would be putting it mildly. Because of this, Tim also had to fall into the trap of doing whatever work came in to pay the bills. For many years, Tim did anything he could just to put bread on the table for his family.

(Please note that if this is the situation you are currently in, we applaud you. Sometimes, life is all about survival. However, if you've picked up this book, we hope you're on your way to more than just survival. If not, hopefully, this book will help you find more joy in your survival period.)

Eventually, Tim became a Real Estate Agent, but he still often feels behind because of what happened in his first career. This is the state Larry and Tim were in when they started talking about this method and turning it into a book for others to learn from. They had many long discussions and practiced using the method before they invited in Dawn, the writer.

Dawn joined the discussion later but has also found insight in using the method created by Larry and Tim. Initially, she thought she was just here to help fill out the writing and do some editing. However, with time, she has become an integral part of the process. She is ideally placed to utilize this method because she is in the process of entering and solidifying her career. Unlike Larry and Tim, she's a little younger. She has used this method to identify and solidify her passions earlier than either Larry or Tim was able to. As such, she hopes to avoid large patches of her life where she feels unsuccessful.

While all three authors can utilize this method to improve their current lives, they are all at different points in their lives. Larry mostly uses it to make sure his "retirement" is fulfilling, and he can look back and see how this method could have improved his life if he had been able to use it then. His main goal is to prevent others from spending so long searching for their passion that they only get to fulfill it in their retirement. Tim is fully in his career and uses this method to keep himself on track for his personal goals of fulfillment and success. His goal is to show that it is never too late to continue improving yourself. Dawn is at the beginning of her career and uses this method to prevent her from falling into the idea of whatever it takes to get ahead. This method will reveal to you your Natural and Nurtured Abilities and how those attributes affect your day-to-day actions. We look forward to guiding you through the process of the Float Your Boat Method.

Chapter 2

A Place to Start

When looked at briefly, the Float the Boat Method may seem overwhelming or confusing, but trust us. We will guide you through the whole process. But before we jump into the complete process, we need to talk about some terms we will be using often. As you probably already know, words can have many different definitions, and those definitions can have different interpretations by different people. So let us make clear what our definitions are for the key terms in this book.

Key Words

- **What Floats Your Boat:** This means participating primarily in the necessary activities you thrive in doing that will lead to your definition of success.
- **Float the Boat Method:** These are the tools and techniques we have created to help you learn to float your boat.
- **Success:** This means spending the majority of your time doing activities that float your boat.
- **Fulfillment:** This means being able to find a balance in your life between all activities you want and must do.

What Floats Your Boat

- **Natural Abilities:** These come quickly to you and can be recognized by others easily.

  * **Unique Abilities:** These are the abilities you are naturally good at using, and you desire to cultivate them.
  * **Talents:** These are the foundations of your Natural Abilities.
  * **Intuitive Problem Solving:** This is how your brain instinctively searches for solutions to problems.

- **Nurtured Abilities:** These are the abilities you see and value in your Very Important People (VIPs), so you strive to gain them for yourself.

  * **Principles:** These are Nurtured Abilities that never waver.
  * **Values:** These are Nurtured Abilities that can change depending on the situation.

We will discuss each keyword in more detail throughout the book. However, if you ever forget or get confused, come back here for a quick reminder of what we mean when we use these terms.

Remember, this process is only as useful as you make it. We can give you ideas and support, but unless you do the work, nothing will change.

That being said, the next details that need to be explained are when we talk about your different abilities.

What Floats Your Boat

Classification of Abilities

There are two main types of abilities that, when they come together, cause your boat to float. Those two categories are

Natural Abilities and Nurtured Abilities.

You might remember these from the keywords list a page or two ago. In the following sections, we will discuss each category in detail. However, let's begin with a brief summary.

Natural Abilities

Natural Abilities are the skills you were born with, such as your Unique Abilities, Talents, and Intuitive Approach to Problem-Solving. Generally speaking, these are gifts you maintain throughout your whole life. You may sharpen and hone those skills in your lifetime, but you are naturally attuned to using the skill itself and using it well.

You find what your Natural Abilities are by looking outside of yourself. This means that your Natural Abilities are found by asking those you trust and taking reputable tests to discover those skills. Chapter 4 will guide you to a few different reputable tests we highly suggest you use. However, there are many tests available. Appendix A has a detailed list of some of the tests available online in addition to the three we suggest in Chapter 4.

Nurtured Abilities

Throughout your life, you cultivate your Nurtured Abilities because they are abilities respected by your parents, educators, and trainers. Because these abilities are prized by those you deem Very Important People (VIPs), you desire and choose to gain them too.

These skills may not come as easily and may require more cultivation than your Natural Abilities. However, due to your life experiences, you have learned their worth and strive to integrate them into your life.

Finding your Nurtured Abilities requires you to look inside yourself. This means your Nurtured Abilities are found through introspection and self-reflection. Nurtured Abilities are Principles and Values that you have deemed important in your life. Chapter 5 will provide an exercise to help you identify your Nurtured Abilities.

To find What Floats Your Boat, you must first identify your Natural and Nurtured Abilities. Once discovered, these abilities shine a light on what truly motivates you to keep working. That motivation is what keeps your boat afloat.

The next two chapters take you through a series of activities to identify your Natural and Nurtured Abilities.

The Float Your Boat Method

Once you have discovered your Natural and Nurtured Abilities, you need to do something with them. As much fun as it is to learn new things about yourself, if you don't do anything with that information, then it was all just a fun party trick. We want to help you move past self-understanding and into self-improvement.

Again, in later chapters, we will go into this concept of The What Floats Your Boat

Float Your Boat Method in greater detail. However, here is a quick summary to revisit if you ever feel the need.

Now you know your Natural and Nurtured Abilities. So, what do you do with them? It's simple, really. You look at all the activities you do in a day and classify them on whether or not you have/get to use your Natural or Nurtured Abilities to complete the tasks. Once you have that figured out, you create a chart to show how much during the day lifts you up and how much brings you down. The goal is to have your days spent mostly doing activities that lift you up.

It sounds simple, right? Don't worry if it doesn't. As we said earlier, this is a brief explanation of the process. We will fill in the gaps in later chapters.

Part 2

Self-Understanding
Natural Abilities

Chapter 3

Natural Abilities

As stated in the previous chapter, we want to help you move past self-understanding and onto self-improvement. However, to do that, you first need to have some level of self-understanding. You can understand yourself without improving yourself, but you can't improve yourself without understanding yourself. Figuring out your Natural and Nurtured Abilities is part of self-understanding. For the next two chapters, we will focus on those aspects of this process.

This chapter will focus on Natural Abilities. Remember the definitions for Natural Abilities:

- **Natural Abilities:** These come quickly to you and can be recognized by others easily.

Within your Natural Abilities, there are three subsections:

- **Unique Abilities:** These are the abilities you are naturally good at using, and you desire to cultivate them.
- **Talents:** These are the foundations of your Natural Abilities.

What Floats Your Boat

- **Intuitive Problem Solving:** This is how your brain instinctively searches for solutions to problems.

By discovering and acknowledging all the categories of your Natural Abilities, you can find What Floats Your Boat more easily.

While many different tests and activities out there can help you discover these three categories of your Natural Abilities, we used tests suggested to Larry by people we respect and trust. The examples below are from the sources we used. However, there are many tests available that can give you similar information (See Appendix A). Feel free to use any test or activity you find most helpful in finding your Unique Abilities, Talents, and Intuitive Approach to Problem-Solving. The ones mentioned in this chapter are a great starting point, but it is never a bad thing to learn more about yourself.

Remember, finding your Natural Abilities requires help from outside sources. The following three sources we suggest are the ones we found most helpful.

Chapter 4

Unique Abilities

At first glance, unique abilities and talents may appear to be the same thing. However, according to Catherine Nomura and Julie Waller, the authors of Unique Ability: Creating the Life You Want, a unique ability is more than just a skill you are good at. A unique ability is the essence of what you love to do and do best (Nomura and Waller, ch. 1). Their book helped us realize the difference between unique abilities and talents, which is an important part of discovering What Floats Your Boat.

However, before you can find What Floats Your Boat, you need to learn what a unique ability is. There are four characteristics of unique abilities:

1. Other people notice and value the ability.
2. Using this ability ignites your passions and encourages you to continue using it.
3. This ability provides energy both for you and others around you.
4. This ability inspires a desire to cultivate and improve the skill as much as possible, even if you already excel in using that skill. (Nomura and Waller, ch. 1)

How do you discover your unique abilities? You ask others.

When we discovered the idea of unique abilities and the benefits of knowing your unique abilities, we set out on a course to learn what ours were.

We each carefully wrote down the question to ask and asked 15 friends what they thought our unique abilities were. The following (Fig. 1) is a copy of the letter we sent.

The Letter

I have a strange favor to ask. I am currently studying the concept that everyone has a unique set of talents, interests, and capabilities that they are passionate about and can be used to create a lot of value in the world. During my study, I realized I would like help discovering my unique abilities. I hope you can help.

I value your opinion, so I ask you to provide me with some feedback by answering this question:

What do you see as my unique ability?

Your answer may include my talents and abilities, characteristics that describe me, what I'm good at, how I do things, what you count on, and other distinguishing features you see about who I am. However, feel free to answer the way you see fit.

Hopefully, you can get this back to me within two weeks.

Figure 1 (Nomura and Waller ch. 2)

Each of our friends responded with consideration and care. While it may feel daunting to ask such a personal question, remember those around you want to help you learn and grow (and if they don't, then you don't want their feedback). List up to ten people you would ask for their response on your Unique Abilities here:

1. _____
2. _____
3. _____
4. _____
5. _____
6. _____
7. _____
8. _____
9. _____
10. _____

So, what did our friends say were our Unique Abilities?

Larry

When Larry reviewed all of their responses, he discovered that their answers came in two categories. One category was from his professional friends, other lawyers or clients, and the other from friends who were personal, from his social life, or his church.

Larry's professional friends responded that he is creative, thinks outside the box, and uses unique ideas to solve problems.

Larry's social friends identified him as caring and concerned. He would shoulder the burdens and help the one person who was in need.

An instance of Larry using this trait can be seen in the following story:

In the local newspaper, I saw an article about a young widow whose husband was just killed while driving home from work around midnight. She was pregnant and already the mother of two children.

They were in the process of purchasing their dream home and selling other real estate they owned to pay for the new house. The article indicated she was worried and stressed not just at losing her husband but also because of the unknown, daunting task of how she would deal with the houses. More than one attorney had told her that it would cost almost $30,000 to sell the houses because of Probate.

I thought that was unreasonably high. So, I reached out to this young lady through the reporter, who was a friend of mine. We met, and I figured out a way to transfer the real estate into her name so she could sell it very quickly.

I was able to assist this young mother through this time of loss, confusion, and trial at no cost to her.

Larry saw someone who needed help and immediately reached out to help. He helped her shoulder the burden of selling a house in Probate. He was also able to use his creative thinking to reduce the cost of all legal fees to nothing. While Larry did this action before he understood his Unique Abilities, it shows how our Natural Abilities are

What Floats Your Boat

embedded deep within us, and the more aware we are of them, the more we can utilize them.

Tim

Tim's friends also responded with many unique answers. However, a recurring theme in the responses was Tim's ability to listen well and respond in a helpful way, which was a result of his broad knowledge and constant desire to learn.

Tim also had an opportunity to use his Unique Abilities before he knew what they were:

In my early employment years, I strove to learn all I could about what I was tasked to do so that I could do it correctly, purposefully, and faster than others. At the age of seventeen, I was tasked with doing the heating, ventilation, and air conditioning systems, or HVAC systems, in 750 homes in a development over several years. That included the design, installation, and service of these HVAC systems in each home. I also needed to teach a much older man how to create these systems for the next two years. I wish I had cataloged my experience back then so I could have understood my talents at a much younger age.

While I was good with my hands and did the work well, there was more to it than that. What I used to think was just common sense, I now realize, was a talent for problem-solving, especially when it came to engineering. I was using a talent I didn't even realize I had.

Tim has always had a thirst for knowledge. This thirst has helped him develop the ability to help others and to slow down and listen so he can continue to grow. None of the careers Tim did were things he naturally knew how to do. However, his Natural Ability to learn helped him succeed in each field.

Dawn

When asking her friends this question, Dawn noticed two things. First, even if you have to ask, it is really wonderful to hear from others the things they think are unique to you. Second, Dawn learned that her unique ability allows her to listen and let others around her feel seen and heard in a way that is unique to them.

As the youngest of the group, Dawn grew up in a time when self-help and self-understanding books and tests were becoming much more mainstream. As such, she took many "What is my personality?" tests growing up. From identifying what color she was to taking the Myers-Briggs test to finding random personality tests online, Dawn took them all and had fun doing it. As such, when she reached out to her friends, she wasn't surprised by their answers. What surprised her was how little she had to think about using her Unique and Natural Abilities.

I never realized how much of a skill it was to listen until I got older and realized how many people didn't listen to hear but instead listened to respond.

I remember as a teen having a conversation with a friend about the boy-troubles I was having. What I expected to be a conversation to help me turned into a discussion about her issues, not mine. While this isn't always negative, I realized then that not everyone responds and gives advice in the same way. I thought everyone responded by tailoring their advice to how the individual they were talking to liked to receive advice. Instead, I learned most people gave advice in the way they wanted to receive advice themselves.

While Dawn didn't know what to call them, she knew her Natural and Unique Abilities from a young age. She credits this to having a father who was searching for these things when she was young and insisted on bringing his children along for the journey.

At this point, hopefully, you have heard back from some of your friends and family about your Unique Abilities. Use the space below to write down what they said.

_____

_____

_____

_____

_____

_____

_____

_____

_____

_____

_____

_____

_____

_____

What Floats Your Boat

Chapter 5

Talents

Each and every one of us is born with certain talents. There is a biblical story that describes an individual who was given five talents, another who was given two talents, and another who was given one talent. On the day of reckoning, the individual who had been given five talents had built them into ten talents, the individual who was given two talents had doubled his talents, and lastly, unfortunately, the individual who was given one talent did nothing with it and therefore lost his talent.

How do you discover what your talents are? The Lord, in Matthew, said he's given you talents, but he didn't tell you what they are. Nor does he tell you how to find them. He leaves that to us to discover our personal talents and what to do with them.

So, how do you find your talents? First, we will direct you to the book *StrengthsFinder 2.0*, which promulgates and lists 34 talents that they believe are prevalent in most people (Clifton 23). No one has all, and typically, they discovered that most people have five prominent talents (Clifton 4). At this point, we suggest you take a moment to complete the test they created to discover your five prominent talents.

However, before we discuss in greater detail how the test

can help, we need to discuss a slight difference between our definition of strengths and the *StrengthsFinder 2.0* definition of strengths. Our understanding is that the author of this book appears to equate talents and strengths, seeming to use the two terms interchangeably. However, for us, there is a huge difference between talent and strength. Talents are not automatically strengths you have. However, they can become strengths.

To turn your talents into strengths, you first need to identify your talents. Once you know what they are, you can build your talents by gaining more knowledge and experience. By putting time and effort into building up your talents, you turn them into strengths.

StrengthsFinder 2.0 does acknowledge that you need to add knowledge and experience to your strengths (Clifton 5). However, we are stating that your talents don't become strengths until you've added knowledge and experience. In comparison, our understanding is that *StrengthsFinder 2.0* uses the words talents and strengths interchangeably.

Knowing your talents and focusing your energy on using those talents will produce the greatest results. You will achieve greater results by spending time growing your knowledge and building your talents than by using that same time attempting to overcome a weakness (Clifton 7).

We have all seen and recognized individuals who have natural talents in any number of fields, such as sports, drama, engineering, and many other areas. We know they have talent, but they do not build it into strength because they don't gain the additional knowledge and experience to make it into a strong, true talent.

Talents become Strengths when Knowledge and Experience are added. To help remind us of this fact, Larry created the following formula:

Talent + Knowledge + Experience = Strength

or

T+K+E=S.

Malcolm Gladwell, in his book *The Outliers: The Story of Success*, promulgated that spending 10,000 hours in any given area will make you an expert in that area. He cited the experiences of Bill Gates programming computers, the Beatles playing their music, and others.

For example, after 15 years of experience as an attorney, 220 days a year, eight hr. a day, 1760 hours a year x 15 = 26,400 hours, more than enough to be an expert.

Larry was an expert as a general all-purpose attorney. But the master of none left him frustrated and dissatisfied in a boat that was not floating.

When he began spending all his time in areas of estate planning and estate administration, within the next six years, he was an expert with over 10,560 hours devoted to this area of law.

Tim spent more than 10,000 hours working in the Audio/Visual business. He started learning the business at 17 and continued working in it until he could no longer, which led him to pivot and become an expert in Real Estate.

Dawn spent over 10,000 hours writing as she went to school for over 6 years to learn the craft. Honing her skills in many different forms of writing, not just one.

By exercising and studying your talent, you will become an expert. It doesn't take long to get 10,000 hours. In fact, it is very probable you will become an expert in a few fields as your life changes. Larry and Dawn pivoted and focused their skills on different aspects of the same field. And Tim had to change fields entirely. But all three have had the chance to cultivate an expertise of their choice, and so can you. Once you have that expertise in your talent, your boat will float with direction and satisfaction.

However, as stated before, you need to know your talents before you can turn them into strengths. This need to discover your talents brings us back to the book *StrengthsFinder 2.0*. We used their online test, CliftonStrengths Assessment, to discover our five prominent talents. However, you can use any test you like; just make sure to identify at least five talents.

After you have identified your talents, list them below:

1. _____
2. _____
3. _____
4. _____
5. _____

Have you turned these talents into strengths? Some of these talents you may have already instinctively turned into strengths. If not, that's okay.

After we took this test, we had to sit down and decide which of our talents were already strengths and which we needed to work on.

Larry's CliftonStrengths Assessment Results:

1. Strategic
2. Ideation
3. Connectedness
4. Context
5. Belief

When I (Larry) learned about the benefit of focusing on your strengths rather than overcoming your weaknesses, I had already spent many years honing my talents and turning them into strengths. In fact, when I look at it, I realize that t

he first two listed above, strategic and ideation, I combined to make one talent, which I call thinking outside the box. To me, thinking outside the box means finding creative and unique solutions to the legal problems my clients bring to me.

I would review the problems of my clients and put the issue in the context of the greater world around them, and not just what they thought was the problem and what they thought was their solution, but what others might consider the problem and other possible solutions.

Often, when they came to see me, they identified one problem and wanted a specific solution. However, in fact, their real problem was something else, and they would be better served with a completely different solution. That is what I focused on and continued to build upon over the many years as an attorney.

Once I identified these two strengths, these two talents, I recognized that my concerns over the years about where I should be and what would float my boat were just to use these and take advantage of the talents I already had, rather than trying to find something new.

I discovered and realized I could use those talents in many different areas of law or professions. I found out I was very happy working in the area of estate planning and estate administration.

While these strengths have been instrumental in my professional life, I would also like to share a story of how they could have benefited me in my personal life.

When I first attended law school, I made a few large mistakes. The biggest of which led to me failing out and having to reapply to continue my education. I followed the procedure presented in front of me without even considering using the strengths I had to help mitigate the situation. Specifically, my strength of Connectedness.

After accepting my fate of being rejected from law school and beginning the process of readmittance, my job took me to a cocktail party at the State Bar Convention a few months later. At that party, I ran into Paul Wildman, the Dean of the law school I had attended.

Because of my job, I had a relationship with him. He asked me how I was doing. I told him my situation and my plan.

He commented that I should have come to him instead of going to the committee, and when I completed my bachelor's and was ready to submit my application for law school again, I should not submit it to the admissions committee; rather, I should submit it directly to him. The following April, that is exactly what I did, along with letters of recommendation from several prominent attorneys and judges in Los Angeles. I was readmitted.

If I had realized the importance of my strength of Connectedness at that time, I could have avoided having to reapply. In fact, I might not have even been kicked out in the first place.

My lack of self-understanding in that instance caused a significant pause in my life plans. Of course, now I can look back and be happy for how things turned out, but at the time, if I had known myself and my talents better, I could have avoided a lot of stress and heartache.

Tim's CliftonStrengths Assessment Results:

1. Context
2. Connectedness
3. Strategic
4. Responsibility
5. Relator

The first thought that came to mind when I (Tim) looked at this list is that I love history. As long as I can remember, I have always been fascinated by the real-life writings and documentaries of things in the past. I thought it was because I have a fascination with human nature and enjoy striving to figure out what makes people tick. I want to learn the patterns of history so I can understand the workings of mankind in the present.

As I reviewed my CliftonStrengths Assessment Report, I was

surprised that the first strength mentioned in the report is "context." The definition from an online dictionary is "the parts of a written or spoken statement that precede or follow a specific word or passage, usually influencing its meaning or effect." This is considering what has gone before to understand what is now and will be. Finding out that one of my top 5 strengths, according to the CliftonStrengths Assessment, is Context opens up an understanding for me in that I rarely do anything without first seeing what has been done, so I can do what needs to be done. It is one of those talents that have become a strength without me understanding why. Understanding the why now, I can, with greater confidence, use this talent to produce better results in everything I do.

This talent of Context connects with the talent of Strategic. There have been many times in my life when I had to combine the information I know (Context) with the current situation to create a new way forward (Strategic).

For example, at one point in my life, I was working in the Audio and Visual (A/V) field. During this time of my life, I believe I was doing what floats my boat. I could have done this type of work until I retired because I was happy with the things I helped create. However, sometimes things don't work that way, and life throws you a curve. Although for me, it was more of a shot through the heart. I won't give all the gory details because some people involved may still look to do harm to me and my family. We will leave it at this: after twenty years, I was summarily dismissed. I was asked to gather my personal things, and a cab was called to take me home. The end. Please understand, though, that there are always two sides to every story, and we all play a part in the things that happen to us. So, I am not above taking responsibility for myself.

So there I was in my mid-forties without a job and a wife and four kids between the ages of eight and twenty-two that I needed to provide for, unable to work in the industry I loved because of a lawsuit regarding a non-complete clause I was not smart enough not to sign. We finally ended up selling our home to try to move far enough away that I could work in the industry. However, it turned out there wasn't any place far enough for us to move. Things said and done by those who dismissed me had far-reaching effects, farther than I realized at first. I ended up having to leave the industry altogether.

This experience made me pivot in a way I didn't want or expect. However, due to my natural talents, I navigated the transition with the help of those around me fairly well.

Dawn's CliftonStrengths Assessment Results:

1. Input
2. Connectedness
3. Developer
4. Positivity
5. Empathy

When I (Dawn) first read my result, I thought, "Yeah, that checks out." Four out of the five of my strengths have to do with relationship building, but the number one spot was held by a desire to think logically and find joy in research and curiosity. I read this information and went, "Yeah, I'm pretty curious to learn more about the people around me." However, while I've had these desires for as long as I can remember, they only moved from talents to strengths in the last few years.

I'll be vulnerable for a moment and admit that when I was younger, I thought these talents meant I could figure out what was best for myself and my loved ones. The pride set in when I started thinking that I needed to figure out how to guide people down the path

I saw as best for them. I had the best of intentions, but I didn't fully understand how talents could be a double-edged sword if misunderstood. Larry had earlier mentioned how he missed an opportunity because he didn't utilize his talents, and Tim had mentioned how he survived a difficult life change because he did use his talents. I, however, misused my talents and ultimately caused chaos and inner turmoil.

In high school, there were more than a few conversations I remember having that instead of using my talents as they were intended, I used them to try and get someone else to do what I wanted, even if that wasn't what they wanted or needed. I thought I knew what they wanted because I connected with and understood people so easily, but I was wrong. I thought I was doing it because I just wanted them to be happy, but I never stopped to think whether it was making them happy or me happy.

I will say I wasn't malicious in these interactions, but because I misunderstood my talents, I misunderstood the people around me, and that misunderstanding led to moments of regret and hurt occasionally.

Once I realized the mistakes I was making, I turned to building my talents so they could become actual strengths and no longer be misused. Through that learning process, I realized that I had a talent for understanding others, but that understanding became a strength when I learned to use it to listen and grow, rather than using it to talk and give advice.

Conclusion

Remember, talents are something you innately possess; however, they only become strengths when you dedicate time and effort to developing and improving those talents. Sometimes, they can become strengths without conscious effort, but it is easier to know they have become a strength when you put in that effort. Remember our formula from earlier:

$$\text{Talent} + \text{Knowledge} + \text{Experience} = \text{Strength}$$

or

$$T+K+E=S.$$

To turn your talent into a strength, you have to add knowledge and experience. These skills take time to develop. We need to take the time to gain knowledge of our talents through study and develop experience through practice. Only once we have done that can we call a talent a strength. And while a talent is great to have, turning it into a strength is better.

Chapter 6

Intuitive Approach to Challenges

The Kolbe A Index is one tool to discover your instinctive approach to challenges. The Kolbe A Index will give you a greater understanding of how a crucial part of your mind works that you may not even know exists.

The Kolbe website describes three parts of the human mind:

- "the cognitive part, which has to do with knowledge and intellect, often measured by IQ tests.
- the affective part, which has to do with feelings, emotions, values, and personality; and
- the less-known conative part, which governs our striving instincts, or how we go about getting things done" ("Kolbe Wisdom").

The Kolbe A Index (www.kolbe.com) measures your striving instincts, which are an important factor in your behavior, in the mental energy you have for certain tasks, and in how you approach these tasks. These instincts remain constant throughout your life.

While we took the Kolbe A Index test, there are alternatives, which can be found in Appendix A. However, since we took the Kolbe A Index test, we will be referring to it during this section and using it as an example.

These tests will help you identify your natural instinctive approach to solving problems. It's what you tend to do when you tackle complex challenges. The Kolbe A Index test is measured according to four action modes.

The four action modes consist of Fact Finder, Follow Thru, Quick Start, and Implementor (Kolbe). According to the Kolbe A Index, "Fact Finder is how you gather and share information. Follow Thru is how you organize. Quick Start is how you deal with risks and uncertainty. And Implementor is how you handle space and tangibles" (Kolbe). To put that into context, let us share the results of our Kolbe A Index tests with you. Remember, the following numbers are on a scale of 1-10.

Larry's Koble A Index

- Factfinder: 6
  - This means that, instinctively, Larry is willing to do his own research; however, if others he trusts have already done the research, he doesn't feel the need to do it again.
- Follow Thru: 3
  - Basically, he's great at coming up with ideas and getting started; however, he tends to need help with the small details and organization of the project.
- Quick Start: 9:

What Floats Your Boat

- - This means that instinctively, he's not afraid to take risks and champion the unknown.
- Implementor: 2
  - - So, he tends to instinctively lean towards envisioning projects and conceptualizing ideas instead of tangibly creating objects or projects.

As an attorney, my journey was a stormy ocean voyage for almost the next 25 years. I was always tossed about. What area of law do I want to focus on? Where do I get the next case? How am I going to earn enough to provide for my family? During the first six years of my practice, I took any type of case that came into the office: bankruptcy, family law, criminal, juvenile, contract, litigation, almost every area of law except personal injury. I was able to do this so well because of my Quick Start ability. I jumped from one idea to the next, thinking that the new idea would be the one to solve all my problems.

However, while I'm skilled in the Quick Start Ability, I struggle in the Follow Thru ability. At the time, I didn't have someone who thrives in Follow Thru around to help keep me grounded. This combination meant I was always looking for a quick fix. I thought I could only float my boat if I had enough money, and until I had that money, I would always be slightly sinking. I was wrong.

My focus was on money, not what floated my boat. I wasn't recognizing my strengths and focusing on them. Instead, I was doing whatever felt right at the moment without much deeper thought. That is what caused me to sink. You will know What Floats Your Boat when you can focus on the right goals.

Tim's Kolbe A Index

- Factfinder: 6
  - This means Tim is willing to do his own research; however, if others he trusts have already done the research, he doesn't feel the need to do it again.
- Follow Thru: 6
  - Tim is willing to use the organizational skills of others if they are working efficiently. However, if the organization is messy, Tim can and will make changes.
- Quick Start: 3
  - Tim is inclined to stick with systems and tasks that already exist and work well. He's not unwilling to take risks, but Tim prefers to gain more insight into the risk before taking the leap.
- Implementor: 5
  - Tim will fix what is broken and make sure everything is working the way it was intended, and to the best of its abilities.

Losing my job and the housing market's collapse in 2008 caused intense stress on my family and me. We did everything we could to stay afloat. We sold most of our possessions to pay the mortgage. We even worked with the mortgage lender for a year, but all they did was string us along until our only options were to sell or foreclose. Our saving grace was the man I was working for. He stepped up, bought our home, and then rented it back to us. This generosity allowed us some stability during this upheaval in our lives.

What Floats Your Boat

After the loss of my job and the disaster of the housing market collapse, I struggled to keep food on the table, let alone do things I liked. Figuring out what floats my boat was the last thing on my mind. I just did everything and anything to keep life going. Sometimes, life is like that; you just have to do anything to stay afloat. However, I might have marketed myself differently had I known what floats my boat. At the time, I was interviewing 3-4 times per week for months while doing odd jobs to make ends meet. I was searching for a job that not only paid the bills but could also offer some advancement. Yet, I received the same answer each time, "You're over-qualified." So, I dumbed down my resume, which got me the interview before they told me the same thing.

I was relying on my Natural Ability of Quick Start and Follow Thru. I was doing what I had always been taught and what had worked before within the confines of systems others had created. However, I didn't realize that was what I was relying on. Like I said earlier, if I knew then what I know now, I would have marketed myself differently. The use of those two Koble attributes wasn't a bad thing. However, they weren't what I needed at the time. If I had known what floats my boat then, like I do now, I could have pivoted and used some of my other natural talents.

This shows that it is important to learn all aspects of your natural talents so that you can use the best one for each individual situation.

Dawn's Kolbe A Index

- Factfinder: 8
    - This shows Dawn prefers to do her own research, but can still accept the word of trusted sources.
- Follow Thru: 4
    - Dawn can maintain the organization of

others but can struggle to create her own.
- Quick Start: 6
  - Dawn is willing to take risks as long as there is a backup plan.
- Implementor: 2
  - Dawn prefers to envision projects and ideas instead of creating physical objects of the project or idea.

I like knowing as much information as possible in almost every situation. Sometimes, this is a blessing, and sometimes, it is a curse. Often, I hesitate to enter a conversation because I feel I have not done enough research to add to the discussion in any meaningful way. Other times, I join the conversation while actively looking up answers to the questions I do not have on my phone. The Factfinder in me is incredibly grateful I live in the age of the Internet. Without it, I'd go crazy and never feel like I knew how to learn enough.

This desire to learn anything and everything was a major issue for me when deciding on a major in college. I bounced back and forth from many different interests: music, teaching, psychology, science, and even math at one point. As I bounced back and forth, spending years doing general education and random electives, I could not figure out what I wanted to do with my life. That is, until I read a single book. This book wasn't written by some great philosopher or leader. Nope, it was a fantasy book written by my favorite author.

It may seem weird to connect a fantasy book with the Kolbe A Index of Factfinder, but trust me, there is a connection. That book led me to major in English for my undergraduate degree. During that time, I realized just how perfect that area of study was for me. Studying English is so much more than just studying grammar and practicing writing. In my classes, I learned proper research methods and critical thinking. I learned how to break down a text, speech, or any form of communication into its basic parts to understand the whole better. I was feeding and indulging my Fact Finder tendencies.

At the time, I had no clue what my Kolbe A Index was. But after taking the test, I've come to realize just how often those indicators have indeed influenced my decision-making.

Knowing how you intuitively try to solve issues can help you realize why you thrive in some environments and struggle in others.

What Floats Your Boat

Chapter 7

Why We Need All Three

Throughout these past chapters, we've discussed ways to discover your Unique Abilities, your Talents (which can be turned into strengths, T+K+E=S), and your Intuitive Approach to Challenges. These three aspects combine to identify your Natural Abilities.

You may ask the question, how did we use this newly discovered knowledge, and what effect did it have on us? Remember, at the time Larry discovered these natural tendencies, he was over 50 years of age and had 30 years as an adult in the profession. This new knowledge gave him peace of mind and satisfaction, knowing he was in the right area of law.

Larry has said he could have been doing and working in many different areas of law or professions. With this knowledge about his natural talents, he no longer tossed to and fro in his boat, wondering if he was in the right profession. Instead, he was able to float a steady course, solving problems for one person and finding unique solutions in the many unique cases that came to him.

It was almost like, because these were his Natural Abilities, people who would benefit most from his use of these abilities showed up at his door. Larry's old paralegal once said that none of his probates were ever run-of-the-mill simple probates. They all had weird quirks and challenges.

After looking at Tim's Kolbe A Index score, it became clear why Tim did some of the things he did. If something was broken around the house or on the car, rather than call a mechanic or an electrician to fix it, he did it himself. Tim enjoys the challenge of fixing something when it is broken. He thrives when he is able to help others. This insight has been beneficial to Tim. By learning all three parts of his Natural Abilities, Tim is able to confidently say he could have been happy in the A/V world. However, since that path became blocked, knowing this information has become even more valuable. Tim can now focus as he strives to find what else floats his boat.

Dawn has seen how her Natural Abilities influenced her past decisions and is currently striving to use them as tools she understands and commands instead of just instincts. She's been lucky enough to be guided by others in her life, and her boat has been floating for quite a while. While it did take her time to figure out what she "wanted to do with her life," she is one step closer to achieving those goals faster than the generation before her. This is because the generation before her taught her to focus on what floats her boat, even if she didn't know that's what they were teaching at the time. Now, even as that older generation continues to support her, she doesn't worry about what could happen if they were gone. Instead, now she knows why her boat floats and can keep it floating on her own even when those who helped her before are not there.

While knowing just one of the attributes listed in this

chapter can be beneficial, understanding all three and using them together makes it far easier to float your boat. However, to truly float your boat, you need to understand more than just your Natural Abilities. Your Nurtured Abilities are just as important.

Part 3

Self-Reflection
Nurtured Abilities

Chapter 8

Nurtured Abilities

Now that you have discovered your Natural Abilities, we will focus on your Nurtured Abilities. Nurtured Abilities are created when you identify a Principle or Value you admire in the Very Important People (VIPs) in your life. Once you've identified that trait, you strive to turn that Principle or Value into your own skill until it eventually becomes second nature.

A VIP can be anyone, but is generally someone you are closest to, such as parents, teachers, youth leaders, employers, and friends. Often, your Nurtured Abilities become second nature subconsciously by watching the examples of your VIPs. You don't necessarily intentionally incorporate them into your life, but they become part of who you are.

Nurtured Abilities are created from the impact of your relationship with VIPs during your formative years.

In the last section, we asked that you look outside yourself to find your talents. This chapter will focus more on self-reflection and your definition of your important Principles and Values.

Every word in the English language has a technical definition (or a dictionary definition) and a personal definition. A personal definition explains what the word means to you. That definition is often close to the technical definition, but it is colored and shaped by your individual experiences. It is that personal touch that needs to be conveyed to those you love when discussing any matter of importance. However, many of us struggle to realize that the same word in two people's minds may have very different definitions and feelings connected to it.

This chapter is designed to help clarify that issue while helping you identify your nurtured Principles and Values. While often used interchangeably, in this book, we define Principles and Values differently.

Principles are rules or laws that are permanent, unchanging, and universal in nature.

Values are internal and subjective, and they may change over time.

The next couple of pages will consist of a list of Principles and Values that a person might have or develop. From that list, circle 10 Principles or Values that are the most important to you and/or have sought to cultivate in your own life. (Also, if we missed a Principle or Value you think deserved to be on the list, feel free to use it for your personal list of 10 abilities.)

No doubt there will be more than 10 abilities that you consider important. However, the goal is to narrow them down to the ones you prize the most.

50

Accountable	Collaborative
Adaptable	Committed
Adventurous	Communicator
Alert	Compassion
Ambitious	Comradeship
Appropriate	Connected
Assertive	Conscious
Astute	Considerate
Attentive	Consistent
Authentic	Contributes
Aware	Cooperative
Bravery	Courageous
Calm	Creative
Candid	Curious
Capable	Dedicated
Certain	Determined
Charismatic	Diplomatic
Clear	Directive

Disciplined	Friendly
Dynamic	Forgiving
Easygoing	Forgiveness
Effective	Generative
Efficient	Generosity
Empathetic	Gratitude
Empowers	Happy
Encouraging	Hard Working
Energetic	Helpful
Enthusiastic	Honest
Ethical	Honorable
Excited	Humility
Expressive	Humorous
Facilitates	Imaginative
Fairness	Immaculate
Faithful	Independent
Fearless	Initiates
Flexible	Innovative

Inquiring	Nurturing
Integrates	Open-Minded
Integrity	Optimism
Intelligent	Organized
Intentional	Patient
Interested	Peaceful
Intimate	Perseverance
Joyful	Planner
Kindness	Playful
Knowledgeable	Poised
Leader	Polite
Listener	Powerful
Lively	Practical
Logical	Presents Self Well
Loving	Proactive
Loyalty	Problem-Solver
Manages Time Well	Productive
Networker	Punctual

Reliable	Tactful
Resilient	Thoroughness
Resourceful	Thoughtfulness
Respectfulness	Trusting
Responsible	Trustworthy
Self-confident	Truthful
Self-disciplined	Versatile
Self-generating	Vibrant
Self-reliant	Warm
Sense of Humor	Willing
Serves Others	Wise
Sincere	Zealous
Skillful	
Spontaneous	
Stable	
Strong	
Successful	
Supportive	

It is often helpful to know the dictionary definition of a word as you create your own understanding of what the words mean to you. It is hard to know why they are important to you if you don't understand the dictionary definition to begin with.

In the next chapter, we provide space for you to write down the words you've chosen and your personal definitions for those words. Right now, we just want you to choose words you think might be Principles and Values to you. We will refine this list later in the book.

Now we know we have thrown a lot of words at you with that list. Take your time and think carefully about what words you want to choose. While you're welcome to choose more than 10 right now, in the following chapters, you will need to specify your top 10 Principles or Values. After you have chosen your 10 Principles or Values, you need to define them. What do those words and skills mean to you? These can be complicated questions. As such, we will provide examples and guide you through the process of how we selected our top 10 Principles and Values in the next chapter.

Chapter 9

Examples

Nurtured Abilities are very personal. In some ways, they are more personal than your Natural Abilities. This is because you choose your Nurtured Abilities, but you're born with your Natural Abilities.

Generally speaking, people tend to be more protective and proud of the characteristics they feel they chose than those they were born with.

An important thing to realize and remember when you review this list is that there are no two lists or sets of definitions that will be the same. This process is personal to you. There is no right or wrong.

The next few pages will be the different lists Larry, Tim, and Dawn created. If the entry is *italicized*, it means the person has deemed that word a *Principle* in their life. If the entry is **bolded,** it means they chose that trait as a **Value**.

Larry

The ten words Larry chose are:

1. **Decisiveness:** Study it out, then make a decision,

and stick with it. It is the opposite of paralysis by analysis.

2. **Timing:** Iron your clothes when the iron is hot.
3. **Honesty:** Someone once said that if you ask an accountant what 2 + 2 equals, they will respond with "What do you want it to equal?" Honesty is when the answer is the same every time the same question is asked.
4. **Honor:** Doing what's right, honest, and truthful even when it's hard
5. *Loving:* Serving, putting others first, caring about others
6. *Responsibility:* If you say you'll do something, you do it
7. *Faith:* Before anything is done, there is faith. Faith that your decision will work, faith that you will be able to complete the job, faith that the person you're working with will follow through
8. *Forgiveness:* Not holding a grudge
9. *Integrity:* Honesty with yourself
10. **Inquiring:** Thinking outside the box and looking for unintended consequences

Tim

Here is another list created by Tim:

1. **Achiever:** When a person looks around to see what is happening around them, many things become

evident that need to be done. Such as the job at hand that you are possibly being paid for, and the other things that make your life better and more complete. An achiever sees what needs to be done and does it even when no one is around or no one else is doing it, and it needs to be done, so they step up and do it.

2. **Analytical:** Life is cause and effect. To be analytical is to look at the why something is happening and figure out that why. Then, determine if it's good, bad, or otherwise, and then look at the long-term effect to see if it is good, bad, or otherwise. Take the time to see where things are going and then postulate what will be with all the available knowledge you have at the time.

3. **Command:** The ability to speak and act upon the knowledge and belief a person has about a subject or way of life. Most of the ability to command comes from one's own life experiences and study.

4. **Communication:** The ability to speak so as not to be misunderstood. This requires the ability to listen to others, ponder, and put yourself in their shoes to understand exactly what is being said. My motto is that God gave us one mouth and two ears; they should be used in that ratio.

5. *Deliberative:* The ability to see both sides of an issue to determine the best course of action. To also be able to express without guile or malice an idea to others to help them see a different point of view, or the long-term effect of an idea when it becomes an action.

6. *Focus:* The ability to tune out all extraneous noise, conversations, or distractions to accomplish what you have decided is important.

7. *Learner:* The more I learn, the more I know nothing. The knowledge of man is always changing and increasing, so what you think you know about the things in your life can and will change at some point. Though with the knowledge of God, who is the same today, tomorrow, and forever, we can gauge the knowledge of man against it to balance our understanding of all things.

8. *Positivity:* Life is hell… and then you die… To look at life and all its hardships can either make a person become sullen and angry, or you can look at life as a series of learning experiences. Being grateful each time you learn a new thing.

9. **Responsibility:** To be responsible is to understand that there is nothing thought, said, or done that is not premeditated. Taking responsibility for our thoughts so that the actions we take are what we desire, whether that is good or bad. We are responsible for all things that happen to us in our lives, and even when someone else does something to us, our response determines the outcome and effect on us. Taking personal responsibility is imperative to our progress in all things: our thoughts, our words, our actions. Each leads us to our desired future.

10. *Strategic:* All things must be done in order, and as such, we need the ability to take the situation at hand and determine the best course of action. The strategy to accomplish a task prevents poor performance.

Dawn

And a third list created by Dawn:

1. *Authentic:* Striving to present myself to others the same way I act and think while I am alone.
2. **Creative:** Exploring new ways to express myself or to do activities
3. **Empathetic:** Listening and striving to understand others' emotions when they are having them
4. *Integrity:* Living in a way that allows mistakes but continuously striving to improve
5. *Loving:* Providing others with a safe space to express themselves
6. *Open-minded:* Having personal thoughts and opinions but being willing to listen when others disagree and change when shown a better way
7. **Reliable:** Doing what I promise and fulfilling all my responsibilities in a timely manner
8. **Sense of Humor:** Laughing with people (not at them) and providing joy to those around me
9. **Supportive:** Willing to listen and accept how others want to live their lives
10. *Trustworthy:* Being a person someone can share personal, intimate details with and not worry that they will be judged or the information will be spread

As you can see, all three of us have very different styles of defining our *Principles* and **Values**. And remember, if the word was *italicized*, it is seen as a *Principle*, and **bolded** words are seen as **Values**.

Larry and Dawn created shorter and concise definitions. In comparison, Tim created more detailed definitions. Either way will help you and your loved ones define your Principles and Values.

Also, notice how there is an overlap in the words chosen. Larry and Tim both chose "responsibility" as one of their Principles or Values. The Merriam-Webster Online Dictionary defines responsibility as,

1. "the quality or state of being responsible: such as

    a.   : moral, legal, or mental accountability

    b.   : reliability, trustworthiness

2. something for which one is responsible: burden"

However, Larry and Time defined that word differently.

- Larry: Responsibility – If you say you'll do something, you do it.
- Tim: Responsibility – To be responsible is to understand that there is nothing thought, said, or done that is not premeditated. Taking responsibility for our thoughts so that the actions we take are what we desire, whether that is good or bad. We are responsible for all things that happen to us in our lives, and even when someone else does something to us, our response determines

the outcome and effect on us. Taking personal responsibility is imperative to our progress in all things: our thoughts, our words, our actions. Each leads us to our desired future.

Larry and Dawn also chose the same word, "loving," but defined it differently. Again, the dictionary definition is

1. ": affectionate

2. : painstaking" (Mirriam-Webster)

However, Larry and Dawn define the word as follows:

- Larry: Loving – Serving, putting others first, caring about others
- Dawn: Loving – Providing others with a safe space to express themselves

None of us is wrong. We simply interpret those words differently. However, note that each definition we created is based on the root dictionary definition of the words. However, the VIPs in our lives and our personal experiences have shaped how we express and interpret the idea of these abilities.

After reviewing the list and examples, use the following space to write your own definitions of the traits you cherish most.

1.
2.
3.
4.
5.
6.
7.
8.

What Floats Your Boat

9. _____
   _____
   _____
   _____
   _____

10. _____
   _____
   _____
   _____

What Floats Your Boat

Chapter 10

Is it a Value or a Principle?

Once you're solid on the ten abilities you've chosen, you must decide which of the abilities are unchanging (a Principle) and which might be replaceable (a Value) from this list over time.

To discover the difference between the abilities on your list, think back to how hard it was to place the Principle or Value on your list. If it was an automatic and an easy choice, that ability may fall under the idea of being a Principle. However, if you considered swapping the ability out for another word, that ability might be considered a Value.

Larry

When Larry looked at his list, he decided that Integrity was a Principle, but Honesty was a Value. At times, the two may seem interchangeable, but to Larry, they are different. For him, Integrity means Honesty with yourself. For example, Integrity means that the money in his attorney's trust account is only used for its legal and intended purpose. Most likely, nobody would know if he used some of that money for other reasons as long as he put it back. However, his Integrity (his Honesty with himself) tells him not to make such a decision. This idea or skill remains with Larry no matter the circumstance. There is no reason Larry might decide Integrity wasn't as important as another word on the list. Therefore, Integrity is a Principle to Larry.

However, Honesty is sometimes honest at that time and in that place. For example, if we're talking about negotiating and you offer a certain sum of money to settle the case at that time and place, that is an honest statement. However, a month later, you may settle the case for a completely different number. This doesn't mean you were dishonest before, but the situation has changed. Larry sees Honesty as a Value because, in different times and places, Honesty has different forms.

In the end, Larry chose Loving, Responsibility, Faith, Forgiveness, and Integrity as his Principles. And Decisiveness, Timing, Honesty, Honor, and Inquiring are Values.

Tim

Tim also looked at his list and decided on which skills or abilities were Principles or Values for him. For Tim, Responsibility was a Principle, and Learner was a Value.

Principle: Responsibility

I had a mentor tell me once that I was where I was because of me and not by random chance or because of someone else. At the time, I was offended that he would say this to me because I was looking for sympathy for what I was going through. I told him it wasn't my fault; it was caused by others. He then proceeded to walk me through the events that led up to the event. I was feeling sorry for myself. As we worked backward, looking at the events leading up to this event, he would ask me questions such as. How did that make you feel? What did you think about what happened? What was your course of action after the event? Through each step, he was able to help me see the times I didn't take responsibility for my portion of the event. He helped me see that in each and every part of the events, I played a role in the outcome. Looking at the events now, I realize that each time, I let others determine how I felt and what I did, even though I didn't like what was happening. At the end of our conversation, he said, "It's time you start taking 100% responsibility".

It has been a difficult path to walk, yet a strengthening one. By recognizing this immutable law and practicing it, I have been able to see my life for what it can be, even when life throws hand grenades instead of curveballs. I believe my father had it right when he said, "suck it up, rub some dirt on it, and keep going." Emotions can be managed when you are in charge of accepting 100% responsibility. This law, like gravity, when understood and followed, can keep you grounded.

Value: Learner

Who was it that said, "Trust but verify"? When it comes to making your way through life, there is nothing that helps you more than being open to learning. With the Internet today, you need to verify those items you hear and read, and compare them with those that you know as truth. When you are open to learning, you are bringing great wisdom into your life in such a way that you will always have more questions than answers. Reading books has been my greatest joy and source of learning. Whether I'm reading a thriller that has details of an Abrams M-1 tank, an operations manual for a piece of equipment, or a book on real estate law, I find answers.

What Floats Your Boat

I remember a time when I was flying home from back east. I was upgraded to first class because of the many miles I flew each week across this great nation. I sat next to a wonderful gentleman who struck up a conversation with me about fiber optics because that was his industry. It so happened that I was studying the use of fiber optics in the industry I was in, and I was grateful for the opportunity to learn more.

We spent the entire flight discussing the ins and outs of fiber and conversing about its uses in many different industries. At the end of the flight, he mentioned that he had had a wonderful time during our discussion and asked me where I had studied to receive my degree. Because I have always done my best to learn as much as I could through books, my answer astounded him. I told him I didn't have a degree and that what I had learned was from the school of hard knocks and study. He mentioned that he had not had a deeper conversation about our topic with the engineers and professors he works with. I came away from this experience grateful that I have learned the value of learning.

If you read through Tim's reasoning, you can see how responsibility is a Principle to him because, from the moment he learned and defined what it meant to him, it became an unchangeable trait he strives to always follow. Being a Learner, however, is a Value because it depends on the time and place when he can use this skill or ability. Tim will strive to follow the Principle of responsibility at every moment. However, sometimes, it might not be the right time or place to be a learner; therefore, it is a Value to Tim.

Tim's Principles are Deliberative, Focus, Learner, Positivity, and Strategic. His Values are Achiever, Analytical, Command, Communication, and Responsibility.

What Floats Your Boat

Dawn

When Dawn looked at her list, her first thought was, "My list seems way different from the other two." While there is a bit of overlap, she couldn't help but feel some of her answers were in a completely different genre from Larry and Tim's.

For example, Dawn's choice of Values, like Creative and Sense of Humor, seemed less than Larry's Values of Honor and Inquiring, or Tim's Values of Analytical and Command.

However, no one Principle or Value is better than another. Instead, Dawn had fallen into the trap of comparison. Comparing yourself to others is a trap that will stifle your growth. If you must compare yourself to someone, compare yourself to the person you were yesterday, or a week ago, or a year ago, etc. The goal is to create a successful life for yourself, so there is no need to compare your life to anyone but your own.

Once Dawn internalized that idea, she could see why she had chosen the traits she did. Dawn was lucky enough to grow up in a home where her creativity and sense of humor (and that of her siblings) were celebrated. The VIPs in her life supported and uplifted her passions. This, in turn, helped her want to do the same for others, which eventually led to those traits becoming Values for her.

Then, if you look at her list of Principles, all the traits listed would most likely be held by someone willing to uplift and celebrate a person's individuality. Again, these were traits Dawn saw in her VIPs. They are also traits Dawn felt she had to cultivate more than her Natural Abilities. She saw them in others and wanted to emulate that behavior. That is how she chose her Principles and Values.

Dawn chose Authentic, Integrity, Loving, Open-Minded, and Trustworthy as her Principles. Her Values are Creative, Empathetic, Reliable, Sense of Humor, and Supportive.

As you can see from these examples, Principles are unchanging. They are the skills or abilities you determine are most important, and you never want to change their meaning. Values, on the other hand, are important but can change depending on the time or place. Values still have great significance, but they are more flexible than your Principles.

It does not matter if your list ends up with more Values than Principles or vice versa. The important issue is discovering which is which. This will provide you with greater insight into how you make decisions and interact with those around you. Knowing this information will help you find *What Floats Your Boat.*

Write down which traits you have chosen as Principles and which traits you have chosen as Values, and a short reason why.

1. _____
2. _____
3. _____
4. _____
5. _____

What Floats Your Boat

6. _____
7. _____
8. _____
9. _____
10. _____

NOW REVIEW YOUR LIST AGAIN. WOULD YOU CHANGE ANY?

Part 4

Self-Improvement
The Float Your Boat Method

Chapter 11

Daily Activity Log

Now that you've identified your Natural and Nurtured Abilities, it's time to put that knowledge towards self-improvement. Because if we don't take this knowledge and use it, then what was the point? I doubt any of you reading this book bought it just to learn cool facts about yourself. If you did, I guess you can stop here. However, if you bought it with the intention of improving from it, this is where it really shines.

The past chapters were about how you do something or why you do something. In this chapter, we're going to take stock of the actual activities you do during the day. To do this, we need the Daily Activity Log.

This is exactly as it sounds. It is a table where you input every (or most) of the activities you accomplished in a day. The following page contains Table 1, which serves as an example. Feel free to write in this book, or you can obtain a full, downloadable 8.5x11 version from our website.

Daily Activity Log			
Activity	Can only you do it?	Does it motivate you?	Natural or Nurtured Ability?

Table 1

You want to record every activity in your day. You can be as detailed or as simple as you want. Just make sure you write a good enough explanation that you know what you're talking about when you look back at this sheet. And make sure to have only one activity in each row.

Then fill out each of the other columns. These other columns will help you fill out the Float Your Boat Method Boxes in the next chapter.

While the Activity column might seem easy to fill out, the

others will take more introspection. When considering the column "Can only you do it?", this doesn't mean you are the only person in the world who can accomplish it. It also doesn't mean that you are the only person in your area willing to do it. Think carefully to decide if that activity is something only you can do in comparison to the people around you.

For example, part of Dawn's job is filing paperwork. She is clearly not the only person in the office who can file paperwork. However, it is part of her job description. Therefore, she needs to do it, but she isn't the only one who can do it. So her answer in the column for the activity filing would be No.

The same consideration should be given to the column "Does it motivate you?" When you do that activity, does it energize you or encourage you to keep working or moving? Or does it suck the joy out of you, and all you want is for it to be done? Generally speaking, if you dread doing the activity or you put it off to the last possible second, it probably doesn't motivate you. However, if you look forward to the activity or doing it first leads you to continue working, then it probably motivates you.

To go back to the example of Dawn filing. It does not motivate her. She would rather put it off for as long as possible. For her, it's annoying and time-consuming. So, her answer to the "Does it motivate you?" question would be No.

Finally, you need to decide if the activity uses your Natural or Nurtured Abilities. Some activities can use both, but each activity should use at least one.

For Dawn, filing is a Nurtured Ability. Her mom, in particular, is a very organized person. This is not a trait that comes to Dawn naturally. However, she sees the value of it and strives to be more like her mom in that area, even though she feels she falls short most of the time.

Fill out the Daily Activity Log for a minimum of five days before moving on to the next chapter.

Chapter 12

The Float Your Boat Indicator

So, at this point, you've gained experience in self-understanding and self-reflection. This chapter will help you most with self-improvement. The last chapter had you list out the activities you do in a day. To correctly fill out the Float Your Boat Indicator, you will need those Daily Activity Logs.

The Float Your Boat Indicator is a table created to help you quickly see what activities float your boat and which sink you. We often affectionately refer to the Float Your Boat Indicator as "the Boxes" as a nickname that is easier to say. You can use the Float Your Boat Indicator or "The Boxes" in a few ways:

- You can create one large Float Your Boat Indicator and place all the activities from your Daily Activity Logs into the table.
- You can divide your activities from your activity log between your natural and nurtured abilities. Then, use One Float Your Boat Indicator for your Natural Abilities and one for your Nurtured Abilities.

What Floats Your Boat

- You can divide the activities based on what part of your life they pertain to. For example, have one of "The Boxes" be for work activities, one for household activities, and one for hobbies.

The beauty of the Float Your Boat Indicator is that it can be used with any category system you want for your activities from your Activity Log. While we originally created this concept to help in your work life, we believe these methods can be used in all aspects of your life. You are not limited to how to use them. However, since it was first conceptualized for work, it may be easier to classify those activities, and most of the examples we provide pertain to our careers, not our personal lives.

The Float Your Boat Indicator consists of 4 sections:

1. **Top left:** Activities that motivate you and only you can do
2. **Top Right:** Activities that demotivate you, but only you can do
3. **Bottom Left:** Activities that motivate you but can be done by others
4. **Bottom Right:** Activities that demotivate you and can be done by others

The goal is to find a way to fill your life with activities in the top left boxes. Those are the activities and hobbies that will float your boat.

	Motivates You	Demotivates You
Needs to Be Done By You	**Floats Your Boat**	
Can Be Done By Others		**Sinks Your Boat**

Table 1

Again, while you're more than welcome to write in this book, you can find an 8.5x11 version of "The Boxes" on our website.

To help you understand how to use these tools even more, Larry, Tim, and Dawn have created their own Daily Activity Logs and Float Your Boat Indicators. The three of them have only showcased a single Daily Activity Log and "The Boxes" regarding their work activities.

Larry's Examples

Daily Activity Log			
Activity	Can only you do it?	Does it motivate you?	Natural or Nurtured Ability?
File Supplement	No	No	Nutured
Create Ex Parte	Yes	Yes	Natural
Phone Call with Employee	Yes	Yes and No	Both
Phone Call with Client	Yes	Yes and No	Nurtured
Team Meeting	Yes	Yes	Both
Review Status of Files	Yes	No	Nurtured
Court Hearing	Yes	Yes	Both
Conference with Potential New Client	Yes	Yes	Both

	Motivates You	Demotivates You
Needs to Be Done By You	**Floats Your Boat**	
	• Create Ex Parte • Phone Call with Employee • Teem Meeting • Court Hearing	• Phone Call with Client • Review Status of Files
Can Be Done By Others		• **Sinks Your Boat**
		• File Supplement

When you review Larry's Daily Activity Log, you'll notice that there are times when the same activity can both motivate and demotivate him. This is possible because there is an outside influence, mainly on who he is interacting with. Activities that involve other people can vary in whether they motivate or demotivate you because dealing with people is an individual experience. So, one day the activity may be motivating, and the next day (even if it's with the same person) can be demotivating because you cannot and should not try to control another person's actions.

Larry's Perspective

To me, my boat floated when I was helping individuals and families

What Floats Your Boat

who were experiencing loss and confusion. Whether that loss was financial, emotional, or social, I strove to help them face the unknown legally at the time they lost a loved one.

Many different activities can fall under that one idea. If you look at my Float Your Boat Indicator, you can see that the activities in the Floats My Boat section are all related to directly talking to others or working on legal documents that will help others.

As I've grown in my career, I've learned to do what floats my boat and delegate to others the things that sink me. Because of this skill and support, most of my activities fall under the section Floats Your Boat. This is because I have had the time and experience to grow and work with people whom I can delegate to when I need and want to.

That might not always be the case for each individual. Sometimes, you have to do things that sink your boat because even though someone else could do it for you, no one else is available to do it at the moment. That's what happened to me when I had to file the Supplement. Normally, my assistant would do that work. However, at that moment, my assistant was at home sick, and it needed to be filed right away. So, I did it. The goal isn't to never do anything that sinks your boat again. The goal is to find a way that fits with your life so that most of the activities you do float your boat.

Like everything else in life, this isn't a perfect process, but it is an important one.

As we close this book, let me (Larry) share a few additional thoughts with you. You'll notice many of my tasks are very, very similar. And as you look over the boxes, some of those tasks that are similar fit in the box of motivating me and demotivating me. The same task can be on the positive side or the negative side. So, what makes them different?

What Floats Your Boat

The difference is the context and the items that need to be resolved in that task. For example, telephone calls. Some calls are just with a challenging person who is, the best way to describe it, a pain in the neck. Others are with people sharing unique and interesting problems, enabling me to use my creative, think-out-of-the-box talents and natural attributes.

Some are just mundane writing assignments, and others are creative writing. And that's what life is: a combination of positive and negative. However, if you can focus on the positive side, as you see from my boxes, your boat will float.

Tim's Example

Daily Activity Log			
Activity	Can only you do it?	Does it motivate you?	Natural or Nurtured Ability?
Personal Study	Yes	Yes	Natural
Sphere of Influence Calls	Yes	Eventually	Both
Call Mortgage Company	Yes	No	Nurtured
Take Pictures of Listings	No	No	Nurtured
Write Descriptions	No	No	Nurtured
Attend Debate	Yes	Yes	Natural
Listing Appointment	Yes	Yes	Both

	Motivates You	Demotivates You
Needs to Be Done By You	**Floats Your Boat** • Personal Study • Attend Debate • Listing Appointment	• Calling Mortgage Company
Can Be Done By Others	• Sphere of Influence Calls	• **Sinks Your Boat** • Writing Descriptions • Taking Pictures of Listings

Like Larry's Daily Activity Log, you'll notice an anomaly when reviewing Tim's Daily Activity Log. He states that making "Sphere of Influence Calls" eventually motivates him. Again, this goes back to how dealing with others can make activities more nuanced than doing an activity alone. Allow yourself grace and acknowledge those nuances when you're filling out your own Daily Activity Log.

Tim's Perspective

From the time I can remember, I have always pondered and discussed the meaning of life and its vagaries, looking for the why of this and that. The study of history and human nature has fascinated me since I was a small child. Learning why individuals and groups of people do things and live the way they do has brought me additional understanding of my personal life and the lives of others. While learning many different trades, I have been afforded the experiences that have given me an understanding of the things of this earth and its mechanics. I have found that reading as much as I can builds the foundation of belief and the path upon which we travel. From this path, I desire to share my insights so that others may follow a smoother path than mine. I realize the trials and tribulations we go through give us the strength and experience to continue in our boat. If I can help you find What Floats Your Boat and how to keep it afloat, I would be honored to help.

As you work through this book, you may find, as I did, that some of the exercises may need to be completed more than once. In fact, I still make logs of tasks completed to analyze and see how I am doing. In real estate, I have chosen to be a one-man show. That means the majority of my work has to be done by myself. There are things that can be delegated if I want to bear the additional cost of having others do it for me. To ensure that every "T" is crossed and every "I" is dotted for those I serve, I tend to do it alone because I know the context of the importance that all things are correct. Yet, with this acknowledgment, I review my systems to see if I can revamp them to make the task more enjoyable or eliminate it entirely. Without this reflection during the analysis activity, I would not have strived to improve my work and the joy I found in it.

In the example Daily Activity Log and Float Your Boat Indicator, you can see that I mention making SOI (Sphere of Influence) calls, which are people with whom I make periodic contact to keep channels open. These are friends, family, and past clients. I make the calls, not to see if they want to buy or sell a home, but because, number 1, I like them, and number 2, to help keep me at the top of their mind if they talk to or hear that someone they know has questions about real estate or is considering buying or selling.

What Floats Your Boat

Consistent connections mean the people I know are more apt to refer me if someone they know needs my services. I have found that it is difficult to start the calls; however, they are very enjoyable when I make them. It was difficult because I would spend a few hours on a set day of the week, and I dreaded making them. Not only that, but what was I going to talk to them about that was not real estate? In my analysis of this, I found several different things that make this easier to do. I found that if I reduced the number of calls and did it daily instead of weekly, the experience would be more enjoyable and motivating. To ensure I had something to talk about, I would make notes of the previous calls to remind me of an event or something that I could reference in their life.

Over the years, I have learned to communicate better with people, even though it has also been a natural ability. I enjoy the time to edify and uplift others as I talk to them about things they consider important. Years ago, someone told me that God gave us two ears and one mouth, and that is the ratio they should be used. I don't know who came up with that bit of wisdom; I am just grateful someone shared it with me. It has made an activity that used to sink my boat into one that helps me float my boat.

This journey of helping Larry write this book has made me realize that I do more activities that float my boat than I originally thought. While I may not be able to write in one sentence what floats my boat like Larry can, after this experience, I feel I am well on my way to understanding what floats my boat in a deeper and more meaningful way.

Dawn's Examples

Daily Activity Log			
Activity	Can only you do it?	Does it motivate you?	Natural or Nurtured Ability?
Scanning	Yes	No	Nurtured
Filing	No	No	Nurtured
Edit Book	Yes	Yes	Natural
Write Stories	Yes	Yes	Natural
Clean Office	No	No	Nurtured
Learn HTML	No	Yes	Nurtured
Film Videos	No	Yes	Nurtured

	Motivates You	Demotivates You
	Floats Your Boat	
Needs to Be Done By You	• Edit Book • Write Stories	• Scanning
		• **Sinks Your Boat**
Can Be Done By Others	• Learn HTML • Film Videos	• Filing • Clean Office

When looking at Dawn's Daily Activity Log, you'll notice all of her activities are solo activities. As such, she was easily able to determine if the activity motivated or demotivated her. However, you may question why only she can do the scanning while others around her can do the filing. These two tasks seem similar. However, the main difference here is that the scanning requires a specific machine and software knowledge. The filing does not.

Dawn could eventually train someone to use the software and attach the scanner to another computer. In that case, she would not be the only one capable of doing the scanning. In fact, that has happened in the past. However, that person is no longer around, so as of right now, she is the only one capable of doing the scanning.

Dawn's Perspective

When I look at "The Boxes" I filled out, I consider how I've changed. When I was younger and first started working for my dad, I would have said that scanning motivated me. It was my favorite part of the job. I could sit in the back of the office and watch as paper was pulled through the machine one at a time. It was simple, but the contents of the documents were interesting, and it gave me plenty of time to be alone and recharge after a long day at school.

Now, after years of doing the same thing, it no longer motivates me. It doesn't bring the same relaxation, because I'm not in the same chaotic environment. I no longer spend more than half of my day surrounded by people. As such, I no longer feel the need to recharge in the silence of my scanning job. Instead, now scanning takes away time from my ability to work on my writing or editing. These are the activities that motivate me now.

I find it interesting how time can change everything. This is why it is essential to continue learning about yourself and reflecting on the activities you engage in each day.

In the process of writing this book, I'm not sure I can say with 100% certainty that I know what floats my boat. I know certain things float my boat more than others, like writing and helping others. But I also know that this is a process, and just because my boat is floating now doesn't mean it will forever. Like anything in life worth having, floating your boat will take time and maintenance.

It's a difficult journey, but man, what a fun ride it is.

Completing the Process

Now that you've gone through this process once, how many times are you going to do it? Are you going to record your activities for five weeks and analyze them for five weeks to get a bigger picture? Or are you just going to do it once? Are you going to come back to it three months later and do it again to see if you're still on track? After you've done it the first time, you should have an idea of what you should be doing to be in the best floating position. And the more times you do it, the stronger your commitment to this will become.

We suggest you do this process at least yearly.

But if you only do it once, you're a whole lot better off than if you've never done it at all.

After you figure out What Floats Your Boat, it's time to make a change. Take the time to figure out what you can change in your daily tasks to help you remain working in the first section of the Float Your Boat Indicator or "The Boxes." While it may not be possible to only do activities that only you can do and motivate you, ideally, eventually, the majority of your daily activities fall under this category.

This will be different for each individual. However, a good place to begin is to let others do the tasks that Sink Your Boat if you can. Because what causes you to sink may cause them to float.

Appendix A

Potential Alternative Tests

- The Myers-Briggs Type Indicator
    - https://www.mbtionline.com/en-US
- The Big Five Personality Test*
    - https://bigfive-test.com/
- DISC Personality Test*
    - https://www.123test.com/disc-personality-test/
- Enneagram Personality Test
    - https://www.truity.com/test/enneagram-personality-test
- Keirsey Temperament Sorter
    - https://profile.keirsey.com/#/b2c/assessment/start

*These tests and results are free.

Disclaimer: We have not personally done each of these tests. However, after some research, we have concluded that they do seem to provide insight similar to the tests we suggest in the body of this book. That being said, we cannot verify if these tests will fit into the activity log and boxes in Chapter 5. We highly recommend you use the tests indicated in the book to achieve the best results.

Appendix B

Husband and Wife Examples

As part of our writing procecss we went through the entire program with a young couple. This couple was a man who is looking for his passion (for work) and a woman who just graduated and started working in her desired career.

Natural Abilities

Unique Ablities

Husband

His willingness to always help others and the ability to find solutions to problems.

Wife

Her ability to find joy in other people's successes and her self confidence.

Clifton Strength Assessment

Husband

1. Restoritive

What Floats Your Boat

2. Positivity
3. Adaptablity
4. Developer
5. Belief

Wife

1. Developer
2. Empathy
3. Relator
4. Belief
5. Adaptability

Koble A Index

Husband

1. FactFinder - 3
2. Follow Thru - 4
3. Quick Start - 7
4. Implementer - 6

Wife

1. FactFinder - 5
2. Follow Thru - 6
3. Quick Start - 4
4. Implementer - 5

Nutured Abilities

Husband

Asked us not to share this particular information.

Wife

She provided List of her Principles and Values, but did not want to share her definitions.

1. Faithful - Principle
2. Forgiving - Principle
3. Integrity - Principle
4. Joyful - Principle
5. Manages Time Well - Value
6. Reliable - Principle
7. Patient - Principle
8. Playful - Value
9. Serves Others - Value
10. Gratitude - Value

The Float Your Boat Indicators

Husband

	Motivates You	Demotivates You
Needs to Be Done By You	**Floats Your Boat** • Commute to Work and home • Spending Time with Wife	
Can Be Done By Others	• Morning Meeting • Drove big Equipment	• **Sinks Your Boat** • Filled in potholes • Corrected Employees • Sprayed Weeds

What Floats Your Boat

Wife

	Motivates You	Demotivates You
	Floats Your Boat	
Needs to Be Done By You	• Trach Cares/Meds • Charting • Talking to friends • Spening time with husband	• Vent Checks
		Sinks Your Boat
Can Be Done By Others	• Talking to Patients	• Answering Call lights • Grocery Shopping • Drivin

Comments from Husband and Wife

Husband

I haven't read to many self help books but I am grateful I read this book.

I am glad the book was short, to the point, and gave ways to not only improve yourself but find out about yourself. That is the biggest takeaway I had from the book. Of finding out about myself through the different challenges in the book

What Floats Your Boat

to find about my strengths and weaknesses to find how and what floats my boat. I'm able to look at my job and look at other jobs and decide if I am a good fit or not to different jobs.

Wife

Reading this book and working through each of the tasks outlined, I have better been able to reflect on my strengths and abilities that I do not often recognize. Life can be difficult, but if you know what truly keeps your life more joyous than draining, everything becomes worth it. I'd recommend anyone searching for their purpose in their daily tasks to read this book.

Works Cited

Clifton, Don. StrengthsFinder 2.0. Gallup Press, 2021.

Gladwell, Malcolm. Outliers: The Story of Success. Back Bay Books, 2011.

Kolbe. Kolbe Corp, 2021, https://www.kolbe.com/kolbe-a-index/. Accessed 26 July 2023.

"Kolbe Wisdom." Kolbe. Kolbe Corp, 2023, https://www.kolbe.com/kolbe-wisdom/. Accessed 26 July 2023.

"Loving, Adj." Merriam-Webster.com Dictionary, Merriam-Webster, https://www.merriam-webster.com/dictionary/loving. Accessed 12 May 2025.

Nomura, Catherine, and Waller, Julia. Unique Ability: Creating the Life You Want. Kindle ed. The Strategic Coach Inc., 2010.

"Responsibility, N." Merrian-Webster.com Dictionary, Merriam-Webster, https://www.merriam-webster.com/dictionary/responsibility. Accessed 12 May 2025.

About the Authors

E. Lawrence Brock

E. Lawrence Brock, "Larry," was born and raised in Los Angeles, growing up in the shadow of downtown during the 50s and 60s. He attended California State University, Los Angeles, and then Southwestern University School of Law, graduating in 1979 with a Juris Doctorate.

He is married to Joyce, and they have eight children, each having three when they married in 1987, and they added two more.

For most of his life, he lived in Southern California, and in 2015, he and Joyce moved to St. George, Utah, to be 350 miles closer to most of their grandchildren, where there is no snow. Those grandchildren live in Utah along 100 miles of the snowy Wasatch Front.

Timothy S. Taylor

Tim Taylor is an entrepreneur with 53 years of professional experience in many different industries. These professions included ditch digging, engineering with high-tech electronics in the A/V industry, and everything in between. Projects like the Deseret Power automated boardroom, the University of Utah traffic Lab, and the award-winning Parade of Homes home theater system.

Currently, Tim is a real estate agent in St. George, Utah, and is pursuing a more robust mentoring audience. He is an ardent student of history and human nature, making this book a natural extension of those studies. He is also an active participant in his church and community, serving in many ecclesiastical and political positions.

However, Tim's greatest achievement & joy in life is his marriage of forty-three years to his sweetheart Christine, their four wonderful children, and their ten (and counting) grandchildren.

Dawn Brock

Dawn Brock is the youngest daughter of E. Lawrence Brock. She grew up in Southern California and loved every minute of it.

She received her Bachelor's in English and her Master's in Technical Writing and Digital Rhetoric. Currently, she has three children's books published, *Walter the White Crayon, Barry the Blue Crayon,* and *Yvonne the Yellow Crayon.* She also teaches English composition at Utah Tech University.

She enjoys writing in all genres. Although her main passion is fiction, she enjoys writing nonfiction as well. Overall, she just hopes that one day her writing will help someone just like the books she reads help her.

www.ingramcontent.com/pod-product-compliance
Lightning Source LLC
LaVergne TN
LVHW021600070426
835507LV00014B/1874